CW00487302

Why We Hate
Cheap Things

Other books in this series:

Why You Will Marry the Wrong Person

On Confidence

How to Find Love

Self-Knowledge

The Sorrows of Work

The Sorrows of Love

Why We Hate
Cheap Things

The School of Life

Published in 2017 by The School of Life
70 Marchmont Street, London WC1N 1AB
Copyright © The School of Life 2017
Designed and typeset by Marcia Mihotich
Printed in Latvia by Livonia Print

A proportion of this book has appeared online at
thebookoflife.org

Every effort has been made to contact the copyright holders of
the material reproduced in this book. If any have been
inadvertently overlooked, the publisher will be pleased to make
restitution at the earliest opportunity.

The School of Life offers programmes, publications and
services to assist modern individuals in their quest to live more
engaged and meaningful lives. We've also developed a collection
of content-rich, design-led retail products to promote useful
insights and ideas from culture.

www.theschooloflife.com

ISBN 978-0-9955736-3-5

Contents

I
Why We Hate
Cheap Things

We don't think we hate cheap things, but we frequently behave as if we do. Consider the pineapple. Christopher Columbus (1451–1506) was the first European to be delighted by the physical grandeur and vibrant sweetness of the pineapple, which is native to South America but had reached the Caribbean by the time he arrived there. The first time Europeans encountered pineapples was in November 1493, in a Carib village on the island of Guadeloupe. Columbus's crew spotted the fruit next to a pot of stewing human limbs. The outside reminded them of a pine cone; the interior pulp of an apple.

However, pineapples proved difficult to transport and costly to cultivate. For a long time only royalty could afford to eat them. Russia's Catherine the Great was a huge fan, as was England's Charles II. A single fruit in the seventeenth century sold for today's equivalent of £5,000. The pineapple was such a status symbol that, if they could obtain one, people would keep it for display until it rotted and fell apart. In the mid-eighteenth century, at the height of the pineapple craze, whole aristocratic evenings were structured around the ritual display of these fruits. Poems were written in their honour. Savouring a tiny sliver could be the high point of a year.

The South Towers of St Paul's Cathedral, built 1711.

The Dunmore Pineapple, built 1761.

Christopher Wren had no hesitation in topping the South Towers of St Paul's with this evidently divine fruit. The pineapple was so exciting and so loved that John Murray, the 4th Earl of Dunmore, built a temple on his Scottish estate in its honour.

Then, at the end of the nineteenth century, two things changed. Large-scale commercial pineapple plantations were established in Hawaii, and there were huge advances in steamship technology. Consequently, production and transport costs plummeted and, unwittingly, transformed the psychology of pineapple eating. Today, you can buy a pineapple for around £1.50. The fruit still tastes the same. But now the pineapple is one of the world's least glamorous fruits. It is rarely served at smart dinner parties and it would never be carved on the top of a major civic building.

The pineapple itself has not changed; only our attitude to it has. Contemplation of the history of the pineapple suggests a curious overlap between love and economics: when we have to pay a lot for something nice, we appreciate it to the full. Yet as its price in the market falls, passion has a habit of fading away. If the object has no merit to begin with, a high price won't do anything for it, but if it has real virtue and yet a low price, it is in danger of falling into grievous neglect.

It's a pattern that we see recurring in a range of areas: for example, with the sight of clouds from above. In 1927, a hitherto-unknown air-mail pilot called Charles Lindbergh (1902–1974) became the first man to complete a solo crossing of the Atlantic in his fragile plane, *The Spirit of St Louis*.

For hours, Lindbergh flew in the most arduous conditions, braving wind, rain and storms. He saw clouds passing below him and distant thunder claps on the horizon. It was one of the profoundest moments of his life. He was awestruck and felt he was becoming, for a time, almost god-like. For much of the twentieth century, his experience remained rare and extremely costly. There was never any danger that the human value of crossing an ocean by air would be overlooked.

This lasted until the arrival of the Boeing 747 and the cheap plane ticket in the summer of 1970. The jumbo jet fundamentally changed the economics of flying. The experience of gazing down at clouds and seeing the world spread out below stopped being (as it had been

Charles Lindbergh with the plane in which he made the first

solo crossing of the Atlantic.

for Lindbergh) a life-changing encounter; it started to feel commonplace and even a little boring. It became peculiar to wax lyrical about taking the red-eye to JFK or to mention a spectacular column of clouds that one had spotted shortly after the arrival of the chicken lunch. A trip that would have mesmerised Leonardo da Vinci or John Constable was now passed over in silence.

The view from the plane window underwent an economic miracle that led to a psychological catastrophe: its cost dropped and it ceased to matter, although its real value hadn't changed.

Consider also the bath. For centuries, having a hot bath all to yourself at home was a remarkable, highly prized experience, out of reach to all except a very few at the pinnacle of society. It required the assistance of several attendants to heat the water and fill the tub, fend off draughts, hold the towels, and proffer the soap. It was a special occasion – like a coronation or a victory in battle – worthy of being recorded in a grand work of art. It would be an experience to ponder and remember, to reflect upon and discuss with your friends. One would dwell for days on the wonder of immersing the body in a warm, buoyant liquid.

Jean-Baptiste Joseph Pater, *The Bath*, 1730–1736

Before the advent of indoor plumbing, having a bath was a rare

privilege even for the elite.

But improvements in plumbing and water supply, expansion in the size of the average dwelling space per inhabitant, and the introduction of less expensive tubs have made the bath an ordinary experience. It doesn't feel particularly special. In fact, it's often a bit too slow: it might be preferable to take a shower instead.

The pattern is the same: a reduction in our esteem for an experience follows a reduction in the cost of obtaining it. There is a similar parallel history for light in the evening (highly prized in the age of candles, boring in the age of the halogen bulb), or for freshly laundered clothes. This was an astonishing, unusual phenomenon for centuries, but now the clean cotton t-shirt (which would have deeply impressed Charlemagne or Louis XVI) is barely worth noticing.

Why, then, do we associate cheap prices with a lack of value? Our response is a hangover from our long pre-industrial past. For most of human history, there was a strong correlation between cost and value. The higher the price, the better things tended to be – because there was no way both for prices to be low and quality to be high. Everything had to be made by hand, by expensively trained artisans, with raw materials that were difficult

A reduction
in our esteem
for an experience
follows a
reduction in
the cost of
obtaining it.

to transport. The expensive sword, jacket, window or wheelbarrow was always the better one.

This relationship between price and value held true without interruption until the end of the eighteenth century. Then, thanks to the Industrial Revolution, something unusual happened: human beings discovered how to make high-quality goods cheaply, because of technology and new methods of organising the labour force.

If you live in a craft-based society, the quality of any object invariably depends upon how much skilled labour went into producing it. In the fifteenth century, swords and helmets made by the Missaglia family in Milan were especially pricey, because they were especially skilled, and produced armour that was stronger, lighter, better balanced and more cleverly designed than anyone else's. This was a general principle for goods at the time: a more expensive cloak would be more durable, warmer and more elegantly decorated than a cheaper version. A more expensive window would let in more light, keep out more draughts, open more easily, and last in good condition much longer than its less expensive rivals: it would be a more skilfully made product constructed from more durable materials.

Sallet and armour by Antonio Missaglia, 1450

The extremely skilled craftsmanship of these goods was reflected in their high price and high value.

On the back of this long experience, an entrenched cultural association has formed between the rare, the expensive and the good, with each coming to suggest the other. The converse also holds, so that items that are widely available and inexpensive are seen as unimpressive or unexciting.

In principle, industrialisation was supposed to undo these connections. The price would fall and widespread happiness would follow. High-quality objects would enter the mass market, and excellence would be democratised. This promised to be an exciting moment. Evangelists regularly proclaimed a new age in which universal political suffrage would be accompanied by material dignity and honour for every social class.

In 1911, Henry Ford started developing the car assembly line, which replaced the slower individual skilled worker. The price of cars came down quickly so that it became possible for ordinary workers to afford cars themselves. The modernist designers of the Bauhaus movement in 1920s Germany were similarly motivated by the idea of creating household items that would be both highly attractive and very cheap – available to anyone, even on the most modest of salaries. However, despite the good

Dessau Bauhaus building, Director's Office, 1926

The promise of modernity in the 1920s: attractive chairs, desks,

lamps and rugs for everyone.

intention of these efforts, instead of making wonderful experiences universally available, industrialisation has inadvertently produced a different effect: it has robbed certain experiences of their loveliness, interest and worth.

It's not that we refuse to buy inexpensive or cheap things; it's that getting excited over cheap things has come to seem a little bizarre. One is allowed to get worked up over the eggs of a sturgeon (£100 for a small pot), but have to be circumspect about one's enthusiasm for the eggs of a chicken (£2 for 12). There is an intimidating hierarchy operating in the background, shaping what we are grateful for and feel that we lack and must have.

The tragedy for our relationship with money is that the hierarchy operates in favour of the expensive things. This means that we often end up feeling that we can't afford good things and that our lives are therefore sad and incomplete. The money hierarchy constantly makes us feel impoverished, while the truth is that there are more good things within our grasp than we believe (and tend to notice only when we are dying or recovering from a bad illness). We are rich enough to purchase the superlative egg of the chicken, but we don't experience our wealth here; we are left lamenting our inability to buy the hugely

22

expensive (but not actually much nicer) egg of the almost infertile and evasive Iranian sturgeon.

How do we reverse this? The answer lies in a slightly unexpected area: the mind of a four-year-old. It started raining an hour ago and now the street is full of puddles, and there could be nothing better in the world. The riches of the Indies would be nothing compared to the pleasures of being able to see the rippling of the water created by a jump in one's wellingtons, the eddies and whirlpools, the minute waves, the oceans beneath one... .

Children have two advantages: they don't know what they're supposed to like, and they don't understand money, so price is never a guide of value for them. They rely instead on their own delight in the intrinsic merits of the things they're presented with, and this can take them in astonishing (and sometimes maddening) directions. They'll spend an hour with one button. One buys them the £49 wooden toy made by Swedish artisans who hope to teach lessons in symmetry and finds that they prefer the cardboard box that it came in. They become mesmerised by the wonders of turning on the light and therefore think it sensible to try it a hundred times. They prefer the nail and screw section of a DIY shop to the fancy toy

WHY WE HATE CHEAP THINGS

department or the prestigious national museum.

This attitude allows them to be entranced by objects that long ago ceased to hold our wonder. If asked to put a price on things, children tend to answer by the utility and charm of an object, not its manufacturing costs. This leads to unusual but, we might recognise, more rightful results. A child might guess that a stapler costs £100 and would be deeply surprised, even shocked, to learn that a USB stick can be bought for just over £1. Children would be right, if prices were determined by human worth and value, but they're not; they just reflect what things cost to make. The pity is that we treat cost as a guide to what matters, when financial price should never be used for this.

At a certain age (around eight), something very debilitating happens to children. They start to learn about 'expensive' and 'cheap' and absorb the view that the more expensive something is, the better it is. They are encouraged to think well of saving up pocket money and to see the 'big' toy they are given as much better than the 'cheaper' one.

We can't go backwards, so we can't forget what we know of prices. However, we can pay less attention to what things cost and more to our own responses. The people who have most to teach us here are artists. They are the experts at recording and communicating their enthusiasms, which, as with children, can take them in unexpected directions.

The French artist Paul Cézanne (1839–1906) spent a good deal of the late nineteenth century painting groups of apples in his studio in Provence. He was thrilled by their textures, shapes and colours. He loved the transitions between the yellowy golds and the deep reds across their skins. He was an expert at noticing how the generic word 'apple' covers infinite highly individual examples. Under his gaze, each apple becomes its own planet, a veritable universe of distinctive colour and aura – and hence a source of delight and solace.

The apple that has only a limited life, that will make a slow transition from sourness to sweetness, that grew patiently on a particular tree, that survived the curiosity of birds and spiders, that weathered the mistral and a particularly blustery May is honoured and given its proper due by the artist. Cézanne himself was extremely wealthy, the heir to an enormous banking fortune. It seems important to state this, as Cézanne wasn't just making a virtue of necessity and would have worshipped gold bullion if he'd had the chance. He did have the

Paul Cézanne, Apples, 1878–79

chance; and he didn't. Cézanne had all the awe, love and excitement before the apple that Catherine the Great and Charles II had before the pineapple, but Cézanne's wonderful discovery was that these elevated and powerful emotions are just as valid in relation to things that can be purchased for the small change in our pockets. Cézanne in his studio was generating his own revolution – not an Industrial Revolution that would make once costly objects available to everyone, but a Revolution in Appreciation, a far deeper process, that would get us to notice what we already have to hand. Instead of reducing prices, he raised levels of appreciation. This is perhaps more precious to us economically, because it means that we can suddenly get many more great things for very little money.

Some of what we find 'moving' in an encounter with the apples is that we are restored to a familiar but forgotten attitude of appreciation, one that we knew in childhood when we loved the toggles on our rain jackets and found a paperclip fascinating and didn't know what anything cost. Since then, life has pushed us into the world of money where prices loom too large, we now acknowledge, in our relation to things. While we enjoy Cézanne's work, it might also make us unexpectedly sad: the sadness is a recognition of how many of our genuine enthusiasms and loves we've had to surrender in the name of the adult world. We've given up on too many of our native loves. The apple is one instance of a whole continent we've ceased to marvel at.

There is a commercial version of Cézanne's work, which we call advertising. Like Cézanne's work, advertising throws the best things about objects into relief and tells us in insistent and enthusiastic ways what is loveable about parts of the world. Advertising is skilled, for example, at pointing out the loveable things in the new top-of-the-range BMW: the cylinders, the leather seat surrounds, the moulding around the wheel arches (lithe and muscular), and the army of lights, skilfully massing their beams ready to attack the darkness on the road ahead.

The only problem with advertising is that it isn't done for enough things, or indeed the things that would be most helpful and convenient for us to appreciate. People who attack advertising get it slightly wrong: the problem is not that we love BMWs, but that so much of our love and awe has been syphoned in that direction and hasn't been properly excited in other, more realistic, areas.

The apple
is one instance
of a whole
continent we've
ceased
to marvel at.

We need advertising pursued with the same sense of drama and intensity and ambition but directed towards biros, puddles and olives. The reason this doesn't happen is not sinister or profound. It's just that we haven't yet found a way to pay the enormous sums required to glamorise objects through advertising in the case of lower-priced items.

Our reluctance to be excited by inexpensive things is not a fixed debility of human nature; it is just a current cultural misfortune. As children, we all used to know the solution. The ingredients of the solution are intrinsically familiar. We get hints of what should happen in the art gallery and in front of adverts. We need to rethink our relationship to prices. The price of something is principally determined by what it cost to make, not how much human value is potentially to be derived from it. We have been looking at prices in the wrong way: we have fetishised them as tokens of intrinsic value, and we have allowed them to set how much excitement we are allowed to have in given areas; how much joy is to be mined in particular places. But prices were never meant to be like this: we are breathing too much life into them, and therefore dulling too many of our responses to the inexpensive world.

There are two ways to get richer: one is to make more money; the second is to discover that more of the things we could love are already to hand (thanks to the miracles of the Industrial Revolution). We are, astonishingly, already a good deal richer than we are encouraged to think we are.

II

Why We Look Down
on People Who
Don't Earn Very Much

We're not necessarily involved in this kind of judgement ourselves, but we recognise the phenomenon in our society well enough: the more someone earns, the more they are likely to be admired by strangers, and perceived as interesting and exciting. Respect appears all too often to be awarded according to earnings. And, in a related move, if you don't have much economic endorsement, it can be hard for your character or views to be taken seriously by your society.

It is not a mystery how this relationship became established, because there are so many conspicuous cases where we find a genuine link between talent, effort, skill, contribution and income. The most impressive examples involve the brilliant surgeon, the authors of *Matilda* and *Harry Potter*, or the team behind the development of graphene. All these geniuses had a lot of talent, they made a lot of money, and their contributions are terrific. They make the connection between high income and virtue seem right and natural.

It's cases like this that lead us to suppose that income is an accurate and proper indicator of the contribution a person is making to the lives of others – and therefore that respect should closely track income. This is the view of modern capitalism, and is the spirit one breathes in the big cities of the world's rich countries.

Such an intuitive emotional response to wages operates with a background economic theory, which we may never describe to ourselves explicitly but that could be stated as follows: a person's wages are determined by the scale of their social contribution.

But turn to the pages of economics textbooks and a very different, far less emotive, account of wages emerges. Economics states that wages are a much simpler business. They are exclusively determined, not by social contribution per se, but by the number of people able and willing to do a given job that others want done. If there are lots of people able to complete the task, you won't need to offer very much money to obtain their labour; if there are very few people able to do the job, you will have to pay much more. But in all this, there is no room to judge the worth of the work being done; the determinant of wages is simply the strength of demand in relation to supply.

Taken in one direction, this explains the salary of a hitman. This person can – for the most exacting and difficult missions, where the target possesses private guards and is protected by triple-glazed Bosch-security glass – extract a seven-figure sum, because almost no one else can carry out such a complex manoeuvre. Taken in the other direction, the same theory of wages explains the salary of the modern hospice nurse, charged with accompanying people through their last days (a task as meaningful as one could imagine), yet whose yearly salary is a tiny fraction of the murderer's stipend. In neither case does the wage have any connection to the contribution being made; it simply has to do with how many people are capable of carrying out a task and how much demand there is for it.

It so happens that in our society, some wonderful qualities – consideration, sympathy and hard work – are fairly widespread. This is lovely, but also has a paradoxical consequence: that you can employ someone with astonishing qualities and get away with offering them very little.

The hitman may have made his money in appalling ways, but unless society asks very careful questions, the world will mostly just see his money and be impressed: they will admire his villa, his sports car, his attractive girlfriends. In time he may even emerge as a respected member of the community, who in his declining years wins hearts by funding a neonatal unit or new brain scanning department.

As for the nurse, however much we may pay lip service to the idea that she's very valuable, much of the time she will just be an anonymous figure in the bus queue; she will not be sought out, people visiting her tiny flat will be a touch sorry for her because the bathroom really needs some work, and her washing machine is held together by duct tape.

When these divergent fates are vivid in our minds – the fêted hitman and the downtrodden nurse – the whole economic system can seem unjust: our minds rebel against the gross violation of the principles of fairness. It's normal if we should then scan the horizon in the hope of finding some answers that can attenuate the pain.

In the history of the West, there have been two major intellectual attempts to resolve this impression of injustice.

The first is Christianity: a doctrine that has insisted that a person's worth has no relation to their financial standing.

After death, a person's soul will be weighed by God, and his or her true merits perfectly rewarded for eternity. The kindness and devotion of the nurse would be celebrated by the angels. Wages can't change on earth, but the meaning of the wage will, in the eyes of Christianity, be altered, and the humiliation of poverty should hence lose its sting.

The other major attempt to introduce justice took place under the tranquil dome of the central reading room of the British Library in the mid-nineteenth century, where a bearded man sat through long sultry summers and gelid winters penning a dense treatise on Capital. Karl Marx's (1818–1883) work argued for a new world in which workers would for the first time be rewarded according to the worth of their contributions to society. Down would go the wages of the hitmen, casino owners and mining tycoons; up would go the wages of the nurse and the farmer. Communism would return justice to incomes.

In their own day, these seemed like very impressive solutions. Yet, for different reasons, they are not ideas we can put our hopes on now. The current economic order seems pretty firmly established and is not about to change any time soon. However, hopes remain for some way of dealing with the disjuncture between wages and contribution or wages and respect.

It may be an odd place to look, but the most immediately usable solution may lie in an unexpected place: the walls of an upper gallery in the Wallace Collection in London's Manchester Square, home to a small painting called *The Lacemaker*, by the little-known German artist Caspar Netscher (1639–1684).

We've caught the lacemaker in what looks like a quiet mid-afternoon. She's concentrating on her difficult task, carefully threading her needle. It will take her around five hours to make just one square centimetre. Her eyes will tire. She will make something dazzling and moving, an externalisation of the best sides of her nature. And the reward for her exquisite craftsmanship will be a few pennies at best.

Lacemaking was a major industry for women in the seventeenth and eighteenth centuries, but also one of the lowest paid, for a stubborn, unbudgeable reason we're now coming to understand: lots of people could do this work.

Interestingly, many artists were drawn to painting

Caspar Netscher, *The Lacemaker*, 1664

WHY WE LOOK DOWN ON PEOPLE WHO DON'T EARN VERY MUCH

lacemakers at their task. These artists had no hopes of reforming how lacemakers were paid, but they had an ambition to change the lives of lacemakers nevertheless. They wanted to use art to alter the status of these craftswomen. By directing viewers to the intelligence and dignity of the craft of lacemaking, they hoped to redeem the social standing of this economically slighted class.

The artists painted lacemakers with all the tenderness and appreciation one might accord a wealthy patron. Through art, we were to stop seeing lacemakers as people who deserved to be ignored and whose low income was any kind of reflection of a lack of merit. Instead we would see them as people full of talent and humanity who were doing a low-wage job by the accident of the economic laws of supply and demand.

What the artists were doing with lacemakers reflects a general capacity of art: to redraw what we think of as prestigious and to return proper appreciation for what certain people, especially those deemed marginal by the dominant social hierarchy, are and do. Art offers us a sensitive reappraisal of a person's true merit – and a willingness to disregard wages as a guide to human value.

Johannes Vermeer, *The Lacemaker*, 1669–70

Sadly, for all the status we accord it, art is a small thing in the world. But the move that art has made needs to, and can, be redeployed on a much larger scale – not just for lacemakers, but for all those whose contribution is not properly reflected in their wages.

Art insists that we be suspicious of wages as an inviolable guide to the value of human beings. They are nothing of the sort, for they regularly leave out of the orbit of status people who eminently deserve our honour. We can live in hope of a fairer economy and must search for how to bring it about, but we should recognise that a realistic path to it is currently hard to chart. It is here that Netscher can offer us such powerful solace.

The way art operates promises an end to a sense of being randomly ignored and humiliated just on the basis of how much we earn. Art is a mechanism for appreciation, and is particularly adept at the close study of the ways in which an individual might deserve tenderness, sympathy and admiration – and yet be neglected by the prestigious world.

Art suggests a remedy for at least a part of the problem of the gap between money and human value. The goal of art is to increase the amount of dense and accurate information about people's jobs, so we can stop using mere wages as our measuring rods. Once we get to know people well, in art or otherwise, the importance of the state of their bank balance will invariably decline, and what they are really bringing to the task starts to emerge, along with a fairer way of distributing honour.

III
On Being an Unemployed Arts Graduate

Arts graduates across the developed world complain bitterly about the difficulties they face in finding employment. They spend long and costly years studying such subjects as history, art, philosophy, poetry and drama; then they reach the jobs market and discover that no one has any use for their distinctive skills and interests. If they're extremely lucky, they may find some kind of job, but it will almost certainly have no connection with what they studied or pay very much. A great number end up making coffee while deeply resenting – against the backdrop of frothing milk and roasting beans – how their years studying Foucault or Herodotus seem to have gone nowhere.

It is tempting to dismiss such moans: if someone wants to spend their time finding out about post-colonial theory, reading South American novels or deconstructing vampire films, then that's very nice – as a hobby. But it's harder to see why anyone should expect to get paid for doing so. You don't get paid for going to the cinema or attending parties either.

But in truth, the extraordinary rate of unemployment – or misemployment – of graduates in the humanities is a sign of something grievously wrong with modern societies and their university systems. It's evidence that we have no real clue what the humanities, including culture and art, are really for. We pay them a certain amount of lip service; we like to declare them worthy and noble and fund a few professors to dig away in their archives; but basically, as societies, we don't know what the humanities could do for us and, therefore, how people trained in them should spend their days other than in preparing frappuccinos.

The problem lies squarely with universities. If you ask these universities why young people should bother to study history or literature, they can't give a straight answer. Fearing that they cannot compete effectively against practical departments like physics or computer science, humanities faculties take refuge in ambiguity and silence, having calculated that they retain just enough prestige to get away with leaving the reasons for their existence somewhat murky. Instead, they make their students perform a range of deeply arcane manoeuvres. For example, a BA in Philosophy at the University of Oxford currently requires you to achieve familiarity with metaphysics (substance, individuation, universals) and to do a thesis on concepts of intentionality in Quine, Frege or Putnam. An equivalent degree in English literature is awarded to those who can successfully tackle *The Waste Land* on allegorical and anagogic levels and trace the influence of Seneca's dramatic theories on the development of Jacobean theatre.

This represents a gross neglect of what the humanities are really for: they are for helping us to live and to die. The humanities are the closest things we have to a replacement for religion. They are a storehouse of vitally important knowledge about how to lead our lives: novels teach us about relationships, works of art reframe our perspectives, drama provides us with cathartic experiences, history is a catalogue of case studies into any number of personal and political scenarios. Like the religions of old, culture is there to have a therapeutic effect on us, which is why it matters so much in a troubled world.

But in order to bring out this therapeutic effect, we need to reinvent universities. Departments like 'history' and 'literature' operate under superficial categories that don't throw the spotlight on the important aspects of the material they are dealing with. So in the redesigned universities of the future, there would be a Department for Relationships, an Institute of Dying and a Centre for

Self-Knowledge. There would be centres of expertise on changing jobs and improving bonds with children, reconnecting with nature and facing illness.

One would still study novels, histories, plays, psychoanalysis and paintings, but one would do so for explicitly therapeutic ends. So *Anna Karenina* and *Madame Bovary* would be assigned in a course on 'How to manage the tensions of marriage' instead of belonging in a course on 'Trends in nineteenth-century fiction', just as the works of Epicurus and Seneca would appear in a course on 'How to die' rather than in one on 'Hellenistic philosophy'.

One would witness a surge in demand from the population at large for the services of people trained in culture in this new way – given that no one currently knows how to run a relationship, everyone is confused about bringing up kids, few of us have a clue how to manage our anxieties and death is universally terrifying.

The unemployment of arts graduates is shameful and unnecessary, because culture has answers and highly useful consolations to the urgent dilemmas of real people. We just need to get these insights out, package them properly, and commercialise them adequately, so that the armies of people currently serving coffee can put their minds to proper use.

We aren't creatures who need only practical things like food and drink, cement and running shoes. We also desperately crave nourishment for what we might as well, with no superficial associations, call our souls. This soul-related work should become a huge and legitimate part of the world economy, worth as many billions as the cement trade.

The sooner we clarify what culture is for, and learn how to use it as intended by its creators, the sooner we will start to view arts graduates as being no less useful than their colleagues in computer science or accountancy – and the sooner they'll have other options beyond the coffee counter.

IV
Good
Materialism

It doesn't seem to make sense to suggest that there might be such a thing as 'good materialism': after all, surely materialism is just plain bad? When people want to pinpoint the root cause of corruption in our age, they generally only need to point the finger at our attachment to material things. We're apparently sick because we're so materialistic.

It can seem as if we're faced with a stark choice. *Either* you can be materialistic: obsessed with money and possessions, shallow and selfish. *Or*, you can reject materialism, be good and focus on more important matters of the spirit.

But most of us are, in our hearts, stuck somewhere between these two choices, which is uncomfortable. We are still enmeshed in the desire to possess – but we are encouraged to feel rather bad about it.

Yet, crucially, it's not actually materialism – the pure fact of buying things and getting excited by possessions – that's ever really the problem. We're failing to make a clear distinction between *good* and *bad* versions of materialism.

Let's try to understand good materialism through a slightly unusual route: religion. Because we see them as focused exclusively on spiritual things, it can be surprising to note how much use religions have made of material things. They have spent a lot of time making, and thinking about, shrines, temples, monasteries, artworks, scrolls to hang in houses, clothes and ceremonies.

However, they have cared about these things for one reason only – because they have wanted material things to serve the highest and noblest purpose: the development of our souls. It is just that they have recognised that we are incarnate sensory bodily beings – and that the way to get through to our souls has to be, at least in part, through our bodies (rather than merely through the intellect).

The importance of material things was, for centuries, at the core of Christianity, which proposed that Jesus was both the highest spiritual being, *and* a flesh and blood person: he was the spirit incarnate; holiness em*bodied.*

In the Catholic Mass, great significance is accorded to bread and wine, which are believed to be transubstantiations of Christ: that is, material objects

We are
enmeshed
in the desire to
possess –
but we are
encouraged
to feel rather
bad about it.

which simultaneously have a spiritual identity, just as Jesus himself combined the spiritual and the bodily while on earth.

This can sound like a very weird and arcane point entirely removed from the local shopping mall – but exactly the same concept actually applies outside of religions. Many good material possessions can be said to involve a kind of 'transubstantiation', whereby they are both practical and physical and also embody or allude to a positive personality or spirit.

One can imagine a handsome wooden chair that 'transubstantiates' a set of important values: straightforwardness, strength, honesty and elegance. By getting closer to the chair, we could become a little more like it, which is an important piece of inner evolution.

Material objects can therefore be said to play a positive psychological (or spiritual) role in our lives when higher more positive ideals are 'materialised' in them, and so when buying and using them daily gives us a chance to get closer to our better selves. When they are contained in physical things, valuable psychological qualities that are otherwise often intermittent in our thoughts and conduct can become more stable and resilient.

This is not to say that all consumerism just conveniently turns out to be great. It depends on what a given material object stands for. An object can transubstantiate the very worst sides of human nature – greed, callousness, the desire to triumph – as much as it can the best. So we must be careful not to decry or celebrate all material consumption: we have to ensure that the objects we invest in, and tire ourselves and the planet by making, are those that lend most encouragement to our higher, better natures.

V
Why We Are So
Bad at Shopping

It sounds very strange to suggest that we might need to learn how to shop. We know we have to learn how to *make* money, but spending it is overwhelmingly understood to be the straightforward bit. The only conceivable problem is not having enough to spend.

Yet, when we try to buy a present for someone else, we can often see that we don't quite know what would really please them. We wisely acknowledge that shopping for others is hugely tricky, but we don't extend the same generous – and ultimately productive – recognition to shopping for ourselves.

A host of obstacles frequently prevents us from deploying our capital as accurately and fruitfully as we should – a serious matter, given just how much of our lives we sacrifice in the name of making money in the first place.

For a start, far more than we normally recognise, we're guided by group instincts – which can tug us far from our own native inclinations. A major defence of capitalism has been the impressive notion that it provides us with unrivalled consumer choice and it can indeed seem as if the system actively caters to every possible nuance of taste. Yet, while seeming to provide for an apparently

WHY WE ARE SO BAD AT SHOPPING

inexhaustible individuality, surprisingly standardised consumer patterns in fact dominate the economy.

Day-to-day, it feels like we are wholly in charge of our consumer decisions – but when we look back in history, we can see how strangely impersonal shopping choices really are. Our desires may feel intensely our own, yet they seem social creations first and foremost.

How else to explain why, in the 1950s, so many people arrived – apparently by their own free will – at the feeling that orange was a properly appropriate colour for a sofa? Or why, in the 1960s, many otherwise very sober people spontaneously (yet simultaneously) discovered they were keen on tail fins on their cars? Or why, in the 1970s, almost everyone in the world was struck by the urge to buy shirts with very large collars?

The choices may well have suited many, but it is impossible not to believe that at least a few of those who shopped woke up from the age of wide shirt collars or orange sofas with a puzzled sense that they had been induced to want things which had precious little to do with who they were.

Yet at the same time, the fear of being thought strange prevents us from taking less socially-endorsed desires more seriously. We might, in our hearts, love to wear a pair of Wallabee shoes.

And we might – if left entirely to our own devices – not want to follow every customary detail in the script of how to arrange a holiday, celebrate a child's birthday or prepare a dinner party, but we may be as shy here as we are with some of our sexual desires. We are taught to think of ourselves as highly focused on our own pleasures, but most of our trouble stems from a quite opposite problem: just how tentative we are about taking our own feelings seriously at all.

It seems we are so much more distinctive than consumer society allows. It isn't – as certain political fantasies suppose – that our tastes are, in reality, truly simple, more that they are hugely varied and anomalous. We might be deep into middle age before we finally abandon the dominant story of what we're meant to wear, eat, admire or ignore.

Part of the problem is that we lack the ability to know, looking back over experiences, what truly brought us pleasure. Our brains aren't so keen on taking apart their satisfactions – and therefore plotting how to recreate them. If one asks a seven-year-old why they like a favourite TV programme, they will most likely find the question irritating. They just like it overall, they say. The idea of going into detail and realising that they find the relationship between the main character and their dog inspiring but the urban setting less appealing is alien. We're not natural critical dissectors of our own experience. It takes a long, arduous process of training before someone becomes an incisive literary critic or gets good at analysing their own reactions to a work of art. These moves force the mind to do an unnatural thing. And so, correspondingly, it feels strange and difficult to comb through the details of a holiday or a party or a relationship with a jacket or computer in a rigorous search for the pleasurable or painful elements which should ideally guide our expenditure going forward.

Our problems are compounded by the way that reviews are organised. A lot of cultural attention is paid to the business of choosing – with one curious and significant limitation. It's assumed we're accurate in wanting to invest in a particular class of product, we just need help in choosing its best example. Reviews don't question the overall appropriateness of looking to get a phone, a car or a hotel at the beach in southern Spain, they simply guide us to the best among these options. So the position of a single choice within an overall picture of a life falls outside their scope; the more complex trade-offs or opportunity costs aren't considered. Despite the plethora of reviews, we lack organised, prestigious support for the existential decisions that sit above any single consumer commitment. No wonder we get muddled.

Finally, though the things we buy might truly be lovely, our pleasure is hugely vulnerable to our inner emotional climate. All the advantages of a resort hotel can be destroyed by an argument. Loneliness destroys the charm of any of the clothes we might buy. And yet, somehow, the idea of our dependence on emotional factors that lie outside the purchase remains curiously elusive whenever we are at the till.

None of this means that we shouldn't shop; or expend so much energy on our consumption. Quite the opposite. It isn't that we are too focused on shopping, we are not thinking deeply enough about what we're doing. We haven't yet learnt to be doggedly precise enough about pinning down our own fun and making sure we get it.

VII
Using Sex to Sell

We are used to the idea of sex being used to sell stuff. It happens all the time, usually around cars, or perfumes, or even less substantial things, like ice creams. It's a sad state of affairs.

Making use of another human being's sexuality to generate an enthusiasm for consumer products seems a pretty depressing manoeuvre – demeaning to both buyers and producers. But before we despair of our shallowness, let's go back a few centuries to consider the educational theories of one of the greatest Renaissance Italian philosophers, Marsilio Ficino (1433–1499).

Ficino was unfazed by our tendencies to be interested in sex. This was, he thought, simply an inevitable consequence of our bodily nature, which dictates that our initial interest in things will almost invariably spring from our sexual and sensory faculties.

The reason Ficino was undisturbed by this is that this wasn't, in his eyes, the end of the story. Though our interest in things may well begin at the sexual level, this is merely the starting point. The destiny of our interests is to move on to a stage of higher engagement that Ficino called 'love'. And from there, we may ascend to a third stage: the longing and capacity to understand.

So our interests are naturally inclined, if well tended, to follow a path from sex to love to intellectual engagement – and this holds true for an interest in people, in virtues and even in abstract ideas.

Ficino was above all else an educator. He thought profoundly about how people learn and how one can best teach people. He concluded that the best way to get an idea into someone's mind is not to try at once coldly to engage their reason – it is first to reach them via their senses and in particular via their interest in sex.

Ficino was employed by the great Renaissance patron and statesman Lorenzo de Medici (1449–1492): both were desperate to educate as many people as possible in Florence to be wise and good, using the lessons of antiquity and Christianity. And they wanted to use art to do this, launching what was in effect a giant ad campaign for the highest goals.

Ficino's ideas lent this educational programme a unique angle. Ficino proposed that the artists Lorenzo was employing should devote themselves to painting

Filippo Lippi, *Madonna and Child with Two Angels*, c. 1465

Titian, *Sacred and Profane Love*, 1514

75

successions of beautiful, or plain sexy people.

We may have often been struck by how many attractive people there are in Renaissance art: this is no coincidence. It's a deliberate consequence of Ficino's educational theories. Artists – guided by the philosopher – were commissioned to use sex to sell: but sell the highest things, like piety, virtue and modesty, commitment to the intellect and devotion to scholarship.

It's a manoeuvre we've come to forget in our own times. We still use sex, but only ever to sell the lowest things, so when it comes to the highest things, we deem them above the grubby task of being sold – and therefore, they languish.

With Ficino's lessons in mind, we should be more strategic. We should recognise that there's nothing wrong with using sex to sell: so long as what we are selling happens to be noble. Indeed, selling higher things with sex is a generous act that graciously acknowledges how our minds really work. We cannot or should not be expected to learn without our senses first having been lit up.

Sandro Botticelli, *Madonna of the Magnificat*, 1481

USING SEX TO SELL

We just have to make sure we're selling the right things, not cars or confectionery. But perhaps things like a book devoted to wisdom and philosophy.

Ficino would have approved.

Picture Credits

p.10 (top)
South Towers of St Paul's Cathedral, Chrisopher Wren, 1711
Jo Miyake / Alamy Stock Photo

p.10 (bottom)
The Pineapple, Dunmore, Central Scotland
Flickr / Photo: Neil Williamson / CC BY 2.0

p.13
Charles A. Lindbergh, with Spirit of St. Louis in background, May 31, 1927
Library of Congress
Prints and Photographs Division
Washington, D.C. 20540 USA

p.15
The Bath, 1730–1736
Jean-Baptiste Joseph Pater,
Detroit Institute of Arts
Founders Society Purchase,
General Membership Fund
Accession number 49.463

p.19
Sallet and armour by Antonio Missaglia, c.1450
Acquired by Henry Walters, 1921,
© Walters Art Museum

p.21
Director's room of Walter Gropius, Bauhaus, Dessau, 1926
Bauhaus-Archiv Berlin / Photo: Dr. Stephan Consemüller

p.26
Apples, Paul Cézanne, 1878–79.
Metropolitan Museum of Art,
The Mr. and Mrs. Henry Ittleson Jr. Purchase Fund, 1961
Accession number 61.103

p.41
The Lacemaker, Caspar Netscher, 1664
© The Wallace Collection, London

p.43
The Lacemaker, Johannes Vermeer, 1669–70
Ian G Dagnall / Alamy Stock Photo

p.75 (top)
Madonna and Child with Two Angels,
Filippo Lippi, c. 1465
PAINTING / Alamy Stock Photo

p.75 (bottom)
Sacred and Profane Love,
Titian, 1514
Artepics / Alamy Stock Photo

p.77
Madonna of the Magnificat, Sandro Botticelli, 1481
Paul Fearn / Alamy Stock Photo

The School of Life is dedicated to developing emotional intelligence – believing that a range of our most persistent problems are created by a lack of self-understanding, compassion and communication. We operate from ten physical campuses around the world, including London, Amsterdam, Seoul and Melbourne. We produce films, run classes, offer therapy and make a range of psychological products. The School of Life Press publishes books on the most important issues of emotional life. Our titles are designed to entertain, educate, console and transform.